Relationship Therapy On Demand

Relationship Therapy On Demand

Chandra Alexander MSW

Coaching for Authenticity, Inc.

Relationship Therapy
On Demand

Published by Coaching for Authenticity, Inc.
3211 W. Swann Ave, #605
Tampa, FL 33609 USA

Previously published as
Trashtionalizations: How To Stop Believing Your Own
Excuses And Have A Real Relationship

ISBN 978-0-9778408-6-1

Published 2014

Cover photo (c) pixelsnap www.fotosearch.com

To the Memory of Samson Yoda
Ganesh Alexander, "Sammy,"
Consciousness in Cat Form

Contents

Start Here...

We all make excuses and we all pay the consequences. Excusing what doesn't work takes its toll, and inevitably destroys relationships. The more we rationalize our feelings, the more isolated and desperate we feel. Every denial becomes a seemingly rational and noble-sounding excuse that is accepted as fact by the majority of people. But just because many people say the same thing doesn't make it so.

Most of us have bought into these excuses. We support one another's and accept our own. Occasionally, if we are lucky, what is unconscious becomes conscious – we voice our righteous opinion and hear it reverberated. It has bounced off someone else's BS meter and its resonance doesn't ring true. Until our meter is on target, these are the friends we need to cultivate and be around.

An accurate BS meter is necessary to sally forth as a warrior. We sally because the movement is never in a straight direct path, but rather incremental, fits and starts that are constantly tested for truthfulness. How does this really make me feel? Is this my own experience or what someone else has told me? When we ask ourselves these fundamental questions we strip away the illusion of absolutes and create a wide playing field. We can make changes without knowing the answers. We can know what we don't want without exactly knowing what we do want.

Every time we move away from what is not good for us, we move closer to what is.

Excuses and rationalizations immobilize us and keep us stuck. They make us victims and ultimately unattractive, not only to others, but more importantly to ourselves. By refusing to buy into words that appease the head but confuse the heart, we choose what's real and go for the stretch. Only this allows us to connect to another in a way that has both juice and substance.

Having a real relationship takes work, but it is never as hard as being unreal. It takes tremendous energy to deny and stuff feelings. The more we stuff, the more anesthetized we become, closed off from anything outside our comfort zone. We panic and shut down because we do not realize that fear is nothing more than being in a new situation. Moving into unknown territory produces a heightened sense of awareness. This acute sensation is feeling personified. This is exactly what's supposed to happen when we get scared – or else we will be somebody's supper.

So...do not run from this. What you are feeling is what we all feel when we enter new terrain. **Until you understand that feeling anything, whatever it might be, is better than feeling nothing, you will never be brave enough to love.**

There is no short cut to this process, but a firm commitment to stop what doesn't work is a necessary beginning. Remember, your excuses are no better or worse than anyone else's – they are simply yours. Does the reason you give yourself make you feel better or is there an aching incongruity between what your mind is telling you and what you are feeling? If there is – feel good – your meter is working.

The following rationalizations are wake-up calls and if they sound familiar to you, they are also familiar to others. We have all used them, so much so, that the majority of time we accept them as gospel. Hopefully, they will strike a familiar cord and you will recognize your folly. Let them be reminders of our humanness and togetherness in this struggle for what's real and true.

There is no need to immediately leave your relationship or move out of the house. Everything, if we allow it to be what it is, moves from darkness to light. By refusing to make excuses, we sit squarely in the middle of our life and reclaim our power. By being brutally honest, we start the process of change and open our hearts to real loving.

1. Meeting And Courting

Things You Need To Know
At The Beginning:

• Men and women are different, yet equal.

• Men are hard-wired genetically to be hunters, women are not.

• A man loves a woman when he feels he has captured the prize. For this reason, a woman should never chase a man.

• A woman feels loved and cherished when she knows she is the prize.

• The things that make a man feel good are different than the things that make a woman feel good.

• Men care about sex and good food and enough sleep.

• Women care about talking, gifts, and feeling safe.

• When a man's basic needs are satisfied, the woman gets everything she wants and needs — he communicates, he buys her gifts, and he protects her. He can't do anything else.

• This is the substructure and nourishment of a relationship.

• This foundation supports the journey and allows each of you to become all that you can be.

He Said He Would Call.
He Must Be Very Busy.

Have you ever not called someone you wanted to call? What more needs to be said?

Death and the emergency room are the only acceptable excuses.

Always use yourself as a barometer. Things that are true have a certain feel to them - they go down easy. You do not have to whip your intellect into believing something that initially assuages your ego.

When someone wants to hear your voice they pick up the phone and call you. Do you really believe that Wall Street mover and shaker who leaps tall buildings at a single bound cannot get to the phone to call you?

More importantly, do you want to be with someone who says he will do something and doesn't?

To view Chandra speaking on this subject, visit the free link below:
https://www.youtube.com/watch?v=4q_mCh4a2Xg

Every Time I Ask Him A Personal Question, He Changes The Subject. I Guess He Doesn't Like Talking About Himself.

Maybe the reason he doesn't like talking about himself is because you just might not like him when he does. The obvious question to ask yourself is: If he doesn't like himself enough to tell you who he is, how are you going to like him?

Being with someone is serious business and you have a right to know who he is — the same way he has a right to know who you are.

We all have a history and all of us have made mistakes – things we wished would not have happened and things we hope will not happen again. This is what gives our life texture, our character grit. When we have made peace with ourselves, we have nothing to hide.

When a man continually avoids your personal questions, it is because he does not want to answer them, not because he is shy or has some endearing personality quirk. A man who is interested in knowing a woman answers her questions and gladly volunteers information that he senses will make her feel more comfortable. Gathering information is an essential part of the courting process and a man's willingness to be forthcoming is as important as the information he shares.

To view Chandra speaking on this subject, visit the free link below:
https://www.youtube.com/watch?v=oZao8HeSeD0

I Want Intimacy, But He Doesn't.

So...why are you staying?

The ability to be intimate is always about us, never about the other person. We literally pull to us someone who matches our vibration. Since like energies attract, our partner is simply a mirror, a reflection of our own openness.

If you are always lamenting about your partner, his inability to be close and open – and yet you continue to stay in a cold and distant relationship, it is you who have problems with intimacy. You need to ask yourself the obvious question – If you truly want to know another and want that person to know you, why do you continue in a relationship where that is not possible?

Now you may rationalize the situation as negotiable needs (better to call it overlapping agendas), but regardless of what you call it, you need to stop complaining. Continuing a superficial relationship is a choice, and if you stay, you need to accept the fact that the reason you do not have intimacy in your life is because you do not really want it.

To view Chandra speaking on this subject, visit the free link below:
https://www.youtube.com/watch?v=eXMTcB0zP2Y

He's Different Than Other Men. He Doesn't Care About Sex.

Is he a guy? If the answer is yes, he cares about sex.

In the most fundamental way, men are different than women. This in no way denies how the glorious differences overlap and intersect, but merely acknowledges that men and women have very different ideas of sex and closeness and what that means.

For a man, sex is not simply a prelude to intimacy, but intimacy itself. Revealing conversations, long into the night, do not substitute for bodies touching and lips kissing. All men, when they feel good, want to have sex. When a man does not care about sex, something is amiss.

If a man is not physically interested in a woman, he will not be interested in much of anything else.

To view Chandra speaking on this subject, visit the free link below:
https://www.youtube.com/watch?v=joB00fTMRWQ

I'm Afraid To Get Close, Unless I Know That He's "The One."

How can you know if he's your guy unless you are willing to get close? Your future is not something out there waiting for you to walk into – you actually create your life every instant by the choices you make in the present moment.

You cannot hedge your bets with love, for if you hold back your heart for the guarantee of certainty, you will never be able to move close to another human being. Not knowing always precedes knowing and it is only this state of openness that takes us from the unknown to the known.

Bravery is nothing more than a willingness to stay present and not use an unknown future as an excuse for closing. It is the ability to feel good without "knowing" just exactly where that feeling is going to take us.

Our excuses for retreating are limitless and if we continue to believe them, we will end up alone. If we are not willing to give up each and every rationalization and confront our fear of letting another person "see" who we really are, we will never have the future we so much want.

Exercise 1

Don't Call Him, No Matter What.

There is a correct way to align with a man's natural inclinations – Don't call him! Set the tone at the beginning and let him call you. Regardless of the reasons you give yourself, don't touch the buttons on the phone. If you keep picking up the phone, putting it down and picking it up again, understand you are being compulsive and leave the house, leave your cell phone at home, go shopping or go see a movie.

Remember, he will call you if he's interested and if he called you once he will know how to call you again.

Reward 1:

Forget The Bubble Bath –
Buy Yourself Something.

Ok. You did it! It may have been only three nights (Friday, Saturday and Sunday) but it was the weekend and this was not easy! Anyone who's ever done this knows what it takes not to pick up the phone, to break the compulsion.

Now is the time to do a little shopping. Reward yourself – a Louis Vuitton purse, a chic pair of "strappy" sandals – stretch what you think you can spend. Add the extra cash and buy something that you have previously denied yourself.

Not calling takes real discipline. It is the real stuff, and takes a thousand times more discipline than journaling, writing your goals in a workbook, or taking a yoga class.

You deserve to shop. Buy yourself something fabulous!

2. The Relationship

Things You Need To Know
Being Together:

- Everything changes; nothing stays the same.

- It is not important to have the same interests, but what is important is pursuing "your" interests, whatever they might be.

- Sometimes you will neither love nor like the other person – that is okay and what naturally happens in real relationships.

- Trust builds slowly. When you say you are going to do something, do it.

- Never go for the jugular. Knowing another person is an honor and must never be used against them.

- Walk away rather than wound. A wounded heart closes and separates you from others.

- Both of you are in this together. Take responsibility for your part.

- It is good to grow together but sometimes that is not possible. No matter what, you need to keep growing.

- If you want something and are not getting it, you need to speak up and say what it is you need. You may or may not get it, but you surely will not get it if you don't ask for it.

- We never get tired of being loved.

Sex Is Not Important. We Have Other Things Going For Us.

You may have other things going for you but that does not diminish the importance of sex in a relationship. A juicy relationship is a sexy one. You cannot trade off having similar interests for lack of a sex life. You are not that easily fooled and besides, it doesn't work.

Sex is everywhere and is as fundamental as breathing; there is no escape. The more you push it away, the more you think about it. Denying your natural impulses, you delude yourself and close the door to tenderness and play.

Once you hear yourself saying, "…We have other things going for us" you need to understand that you have already bought into an unspoken agenda – denying feelings and maintaining status quo. Regardless of the reasons you give yourself, feeling sexually disconnected produces a wide rift, not only with the man in your life, but more importantly, with yourself.

To view Chandra speaking on this subject, visit the free link below:
https://www.youtube.com/watch?v=joB00fTMRWQ

I'm Afraid To Feel Good.
Nothing Lasts Forever.

That's right. Nothing lasts forever, nothing. So now that you know that, maybe you can just enjoy your life when you're feeling good.

Nothing stays the same; everything changes. This intrinsic movement of flux will never be any different than it is at this moment. This is reality, and when you use 'what is' as an excuse to wallow in cynicism, you not only deny the inherent nature of the universe, but more importantly, your right to joy.

In truth, this is not about the ever-changing world, but about you. Unless you can accept feeling good, you will never be able to love and be loved. When you can enjoy each encounter, moment by moment, you will experience yourself as loveable – knowing and loving it will never be the same.

He Doesn't Believe In Birthdays And Valentine's Day, But I Know He Loves Me.

He may say these special days mean nothing to him, but that's beside the point. Do they mean something to you? Because if they do and you have let him know that, and still he forgets...what more is there to say?

A very important part of loving is caring – caring what is important to the other person and making that important to you. Narcissistic people think everyone looks at the world the same way that they do...and if they don't, they should. But real loving is the opposite of this.

When a man loves a woman he wants her to feel good and he is always looking for things to do to make her feel that way. A birthday, Valentine's Day, an anniversary, is an opportunity for a man to show a woman how much he loves her. Why would someone who really cares pass that up?

To view Chandra speaking on this subject, visit the free link below:
https://www.youtube.com/watch?v=gdHI909F-Lc

I've Never Met His Family Or Friends,But I Guess That's Not Important As Long As We're Together.

When a man is proud of being with you he wants you to meet the people who are important to him – he wants to show you off. He "knows" you are the prize and he wants all those he cares about to know it too.

A man who is certain he wants you in his life is not shy or reticent. He does not hesitate to arrange dates with his family and friends, even before he has met yours. He is not protecting himself and "declares" his intentions by including you in all that he does. He wants everyone he loves to see you the same way he does, and he takes every opportunity to show them how he feels about you.

It's important to meet his family and friends. They need to know you, just as you need to know them. If you are going to be with this man you will most likely be with these people, so you might as well start getting to know them right now.

To view Chandra speaking on this subject, visit the free link below:
https://www.youtube.com/watch?v=eRyvsqkAuqw
and Part 2, Questions and Answers
https://www.youtube.com/watch?v=bc2jIqG5ejE

His Constant Criticism Hurts Me, But He Says It's For My Own Good And That I'm Being Too Sensitive.

If something doesn't feel good, it probably isn't.

Is it really that hard to tell the difference between something that has a sting and something that is delivered with love – I don't think so. Don't you instinctually know how something is given and on a gut level respond in kind? You know because of how you feel (not because of what someone has told you), and you need to trust the feeling.

All of us want to be loved and are always hoping for the best.

You anticipate your guy saying nice things because that's what you want. You don't expect to feel wounded, so when you do, you need to address it. Don't sweep it under the rug and pretend it doesn't bother you. Addressing it is how you keep your dignity and sense of self. It is never okay – for any reason – for one person to diminish another and you firmly need to set your boundaries – "You may not talk to me that way."

Exercise 2

The Middle Of The Floor

1. Sit down in the middle of the floor.

2. Feel what you are afraid of feeling.

3. Invite the "creepies" in.

4. As the thoughts come across your mind, simply watch, like you would a movie, knowing that you are not the movie you are watching.

(Surprise – You are not your thoughts.)

When you are brave enough to feel what scares you, you stop projecting your stuff onto your partner. This is when the relationship really starts getting good.

To view Chandra speaking on this subject, visit the free link below:
https://www.youtube.com/watch?v=G9-I-eCTPK0

Reward 2:

Take A Course –
Anything Your Heart Desires!

Facing your demons is not for the faint of heart. This is where we make the cut – separating the men from the boys. (Hey Ladies...let's take their phrase when it applies!)

Remember, when you feel what scares you, you are never the same. Looking the "creepies" in the eye makes you brave and powerful. Once you have sat with aloneness and not run, you can do anything.

Now is the time to do what you have always talked about doing but never done. You can do it! Go ahead – take those flying lessons and start singing! Someone's in a rock band and someone's flying planes; it might as well be you!

3. To Leave Or To Stay

Things You Need To Know Staying And Leaving:

• Staying and leaving must never be conditional.

• You need to stay when that is where you want to be and you need to leave when you know it's time to move on.

• Leaving only frees you if you are free before you leave.

• When you want to run and instead stay, you are often rewarded with something good and unexpected.

• We love the most the ones that stay.

• Always leave with dignity.... for who you are at this moment and who you are going forward.

• Remember you've loved and been intimate with this person.

• If you leave as a victim, it is not the time to go.

• Know that for the time you were together it was a match.

• Only leave when you are certain you will not repeat the same stuff.

Being With Someone Is Better Than Being Alone.

There is really only one good reason to be with anyone – you feel good being around that person and you want that feeling to continue. The minute you choose out of fear rather than love, you stop loving.

Being alone is bittersweet, part of the human condition, but the loneliness of pretending to love is poison. It contaminates all that it touches and shuts our hearts so that we don't feel. Without feeling, we go through the motions but there is hollowness in all that we do.

Being with someone, "anyone," is not better than being alone. Being alone has integrity and honors the heart. It sends a message to the universe that says, "I will not give in to my fears. I am open and ready for love."

To view Chandra speaking on this subject, visit the free link below:
https://www.youtube.com/watch?v=PKra0Vbc6XY

He's Not A Good Husband, But He's A Good Father.

It is a wonderful thing to be good father and certainly when you have children to think about, an important component of a relationship. But a loving father does not a loving husband make.

You are living your life with this man as his wife. You cannot trade his good deeds as a father for his inability to be a good husband.

Acknowledging your unhappiness is the beginning. Do not feel that you have to immediately do something drastic. It is enough now to know the status quo is not enough and that you are willing to do something different. The biggest change you can make is to feel; vulnerability leads to openness and openness invites a new beginning.

When you stop denying your feelings, you know what you need and start asking for it.

I Wish I Felt More Passionate, But Passion Diminishes Over Time.

This is absolutely not what happens. The true nature of passion is increase, i.e., it feeds on itself. To feel passion, you must be passion. A passionate relationship thrives in wide-open spaces; the moment either of you close, passion diminishes.

At the beginning of a relationship there is innocence; we rush towards each other unaware that the proximity may waken sleeping demons. Face to face with our stuff, we are scared and vulnerable. The unconscious has become conscious and now we get to make a choice: Do we blame the other person for our discomfort, or do we accept what is ours and deal with it?

It takes courage to feel these uncomfortable feelings. If you chose to deny them, (the reasons you give yourself do not matter) your heart will close; and the price you pay will be your passion.

So, be brave. When you want to blame, don't, and when you want to run, stay. Staying connected to what's real keeps you open and keeps the juices flowing. This is the key to a passionate relationship.

To view Chandra speaking on this subject, visit the free link below:
https://www.youtube.com/watch?v=opv9Yr0iaU0

He Says I'm The Best Thing That Has Ever Happened To Him, But He Doesn't Want An Exclusive Relationship.

Now you may be the cat's meow, but if he doesn't want a committed relationship with you and that's what you want, he probably is not the guy for you. You cannot make a man want you! Either he does or he doesn't and when he does you are not confused and he certainly is not.

Women don't give men enough credit – they are really pretty smart and very adept at getting what they want. Men are naturally proprietary and instantly focus on the goal once they know where they want to go. A man who thinks you are the best thing going wants to tie it up. He doesn't want competition – he wants you all to himself. He doesn't need you to suggest (or worse) demand a commitment.

An exclusive relationship happens naturally. You know you are the best thing that's ever happened to him, not because he tells you, but because he makes you feel that every day.

I'm Really Not Happy, But I'll Just Let Some Time Pass And See What Happens.

It is important to understand that time is both formless and neutral, and does nothing but pass. Things do not get better with time. The greater probability is that your situation will become worse if what you currently have is not good. And that is because, left alone, things naturally become more of what they already are. That means that if you continue doing the same things, you will get the same results.

Everything has momentum; nothing stays the same. By the time you realize you are "not happy," there is a history, a backlog of images and feelings that have brought you to this place. In other words, the hard wiring is set and has a life of its own. This accumulation of energy has mass and speed and is moving in a particular direction. If ignored, it continues to accelerate.

Pushing these unpleasant feelings away never works. It's like saying, "Don't think of a monkey" – a monkey is all you think of. The more you push against something, the bigger it becomes.

There is only one way for things to be different — you need to do something other than what you have been doing. And if you have been ignoring your feelings, you need to stop doing that. Simply by feeling, you shift directions and halt the forward momentum. Now you have a real opportunity to make time work for you.

Exercise 3

Zip It And Stop Telling Everyone Your Story.

I am sure there is not one thing you can say that you have not already said. You keep telling your story over and over again to gain consensus for your point of view – this behavior is about being right, not feeling right. Regardless of how abusive your story might it, it is self-abuse to keep telling it. The more you tell it, the more you feel like a victim and the more hard-wired it becomes. Repeating your story adds energy to the dysfunction. As it gathers momentum, it further cements what doesn't work.

The discipline is to talk only to your mate and no one else (except a professional).

Reward 3:

Softness And Power

If you have really stopped calling and complaining to all who will listen, and have succeeded in putting a lid on the repetitive and incessant chatter, you will instantly feel the difference.

Talking only to your mate brings its own reward. Rather than having to prove your point, which makes you hard, you listen and feel soft.

An amazing thing happens when you stop the compulsive babble and start listening – you hear things you have never heard before (even though they have been said), and you are open to learning new things about yourself. Suddenly, you feel empowered as this process re-connects you to what's real – you are no longer in your head, talking about what is wrong; you are present, doing something about it.

Softness and power – it doesn't get much better than this!

4. Breaking Up

Things You Need To Know
Parting Ways:

• Words have the power to wound. Choose them very carefully.

• Once said, unkind things are hard to take back.

• Maybe you both just did the best you could.

• When splitting possessions, if you give him some of the things he wants, he will give you some of the things you want.

• Remember you've loved and been intimate with this person.

• Regardless of the circumstances, you will feel like you've failed – this is natural because we all want so much for love to work for us.

• The unknown is scary but not as scary as becoming less in order to stay.

• Give him the couch; you'll get a life. Nature abhors a vacuum. You will have everything you need.

• Remember you chose this relationship and now you are choosing to leave. You do not have to make the relationship bad in order to go.

• Vulnerability keeps you from shutting down. Have boundaries, but keep your heart open.

I Know What To Do.
I Just Have To Do It.

You really do not know what to do, because if you really knew what to do, you would have done it already. When you hear yourself say, "I know what to do – I just have to do it," tell yourself that saying that keeps you stuck.

You deceive yourself thinking that just because you understand something intellectually, you know it. But there is only one way to know something, anything, and that is to unequivocally know it with the inner self. When your own voice is loud and clear (all the other voices in your head are quiet), only then do you know.

Even though you may be scared, when you know what to do, you do it. You may be sad, in pain, but you are not confused—and that knowing elicits direct, swift action.

As long as you rationalize an undesirable situation so you can stay, you will never do what you need to do to leave.

I'd Say How I Feel, But It Would Hurt His Feelings.

If you don't tell him it will hurt his soul.

Each one of us has a right to know the truth. When you hide your feelings and tell yourself it is because you are protecting him, you are deceiving yourself.

We all need to make decisions based on good information and when you purposely keep that hidden from the other person, you are being narcissistic and manipulative.

Now you may tell yourself (and your friends) that you are sparing him heartache, but the truth is you are sparing yourself. Something in you knows that if you say how you feel, something might change, and you are not yet ready to make a move. You are so afraid of disturbing the status quo that you convince yourself you are doing something noble by not sharing your feelings.

But real relationships have honor and dignity. We need to want the same thing for someone else that we want for ourselves; and if we are honest, we want to know the truth.

So, regardless of how scared you are, speak gently from the heart. This is what loving is all about.

Now Is Not A Good Time To Talk.
I'll Wait Until Later.

The moment you think now is not a good time to talk, it's best to start talking pretty soon. Saying these words signals a time of fruition, a ripe moment when things have come to the surface, and if you start giving yourself reasons why another time is better, you are partitioning a life that is naturally connected and whole. Once you do this, things close across the board.

Scared, you tell yourself you have to wait until he is relaxed, the children have gone to bed, and the bills have been paid. A button has been pushed and you are overwhelmed with feelings. You say whatever you need to say to convince yourself that now is not the right time. But if it were not, you would not be so consumed with the need to push these feelings away.

So, you speak.

This does not mean you scream your demands, but rather you find a way to say how you feel. You do not need an immediate answer. All that is required is the desire to feel right rather than be right.

I'll Move Out...
As Soon As I Have Enough Money.

How much is enough and do you have a plan for getting what you need? If you do not know exactly how much you will need to leave and you do not have a specific plan for getting it, your staying or leaving has nothing to do with money.

You are right in assuming things will be different if and when you leave – but that is what happens when things change. If you are afraid to go, you will cling to any reason for staying and money is as good as any. But when you want to leave, really want to leave, something more than money motivates you.

Knowing what you need always buys you more than money could buy.

Unless I Hear All The Details, I Can't Move On.

The reason you can't move on is because you are listening to all the details.

To make the assumption that the more "facts" you gather, the closer you will be to the truth, is not correct.

Wanting to know all the details is different than knowing the truth. Unlike the details, the truth is not compulsive. When we hear what we need to hear, we do not need to hear it over and over again. There is a resolute quality to the truth – we can live with it even though it hurts. Once heard, it is enough.

This is different than being tortured by details!

If you are honest with yourself, you will admit that every hard won detail makes you feel the same as every other - badly. Hearing the same old story over and over again is an addiction. It is a form of self-abuse that will keep you stuck, and you will never have a chance to do it right.

Exercise 4:

The Match Game

There is no limit to the amount of times you can be in a relationship and break up. The universe is infinite and does not care how long it takes you to "get it." It is best to learn lessons quickly while you still look good in your clothes.

Every time you hear yourself say, "I don't know why I was with him – it was never a match," tell yourself it was a good match for the time you were together.

Example: She says he is incapable of intimacy and that she wants it. She has been complaining about this for three years. This is a good match. Neither one really wants real closeness. If she did, she would have left already.

The "match game" helps you take responsibility for your actions so that you do not make the same mistakes twice. It keeps you from being a victim and blaming others. Most important, it gives you new and important knowledge about yourself going forward.

Reward 4:

Go Out with Friends – Have Fun! You Never Know What Might Happen!

When a relationship ends, we often are confused and angry. The more we try and convince ourselves it was a bad match, the longer it takes it heal. Moving on is only possible when we take responsibility for all our relationships, even the ones that ostensibly make no sense. We admit our mistakes, know we chose then and most importantly, know we will choose differently in the future.

Once this occurs, we have a real opportunity for something new and healthy.

So go out – have some fun! Nothing is more attractive than a confident woman. You may not know exactly what you want, but you sure know what you don't want. You do not have to worry if someone will find you interesting or appealing; you will pull to you your match just like you did before - only this time it will be different.

Knowing you have the power to walk away as well as walk towards - take the place by storm!

5. Starting Over

Things You Need To Know
Beginning Again:

• There are good men everywhere.

• If you feel soft rather than hard, that is good.

• You will pull to you what you are.

• If you want something different, you need to be something different.

• Without discipline, it is impossible to change.

• Rather than visualize the man of your dreams, feel what that feels like.

• Be open to getting a match for those feelings, regardless of the package.

• You can't talk yourself into chemistry no matter how much money he has.

• In all good relationships, people have fun.

• Don't make the same mistakes you made before.

There Aren't Any Good Men Out There.

Good men are everywhere – there is no need to worry.

If the men you meet are not up to snuff, remember you have attracted them and you can just as easily walk away – you have the legs and you have the choice. Complaining never absolves you of responsibility but almost always keeps you from the "good men."

Even if you have to "admit" that you really don't mean it – and yes, there are some good ones out there – it is never smart to say this stuff anyway. Saying it reinforces your defenses and makes you a victim of some group that has no idea how you feel. When you go out into the world feeling this way, your thoughts actually enter a room before you and create a barrier between you and the good men. They can't see you and you can't see them.

I promise you – there really are good ones out there. They know they are good and will only be attracted to you if you can recognize who they are.

To view Chandra speaking on this subject, visit the free link below:
https://www.youtube.com/watch?v=oZao8HeSeD0

I've Decided Never To Get Married Again.

If you've learned what you needed to learn from your last relationship – that it is you and not the institution of marriage that is responsible for creating your life – why should it make a difference whether or not you get married again? You will be fine regardless; it will not matter to you. If you are not going to make the same mistakes twice, why only marry once?

Making a decision to never marry again is always preceded by a chain of several other thoughts — I don't need anyone. Nothing lasts forever. Passion diminishes over time – this is the nonsense we tell ourselves to feel safe and protected. But these thoughts separate us from others and keep us isolated and alone.

Closing to the possibility of ever marrying again, you close to many other possibilities as well. When you are open to whatever comes your way – married, not married – you have made peace with your demons and are ready to move on.

You have just increased your odds for a really good life.

If I Don't Expect Anything, I'll Never Be Disappointed.

It is one thing to be open to whatever comes down the pike and it is another to feel nothing ever will. When our emphasis is on not being disappointed, that fear colors all that we do and sets the arena for all that comes to us. If we are bitter because we have not gotten what we want, that bitterness pushes all sweetness away.

Being disappointed is always the result of not living in the present moment. It is about dwelling on the past and fantasizing about the future – an idea you have in your head, a way you think things should be. It is impossible to not be disappointed when you have an agenda running.

Regardless of what happens (and it could be something new that just might be in your best interest), when you have a particular way you want things to be, you cannot see things as they really are and as a result, are not open to new possibilities.

Unless you are willing to stay present, you will never have something greater than what you have imagined.

I Really Don't Need A Man.
My Girlfriends Are Enough.

Is there anything wrong with having both a man and girlfriends in your life? The two are not mutually exclusive and when viewed correctly, each contributes something distinctive but equally important.

We often make this statement when we've expected the man in our life to be like our girlfriends – and then realize he is not. This is not the man's fault, but we blame him just the same. We think there is something wrong with him when he refuses to behave like our girlfriends.

But men are different than women, and if you are smart, you do not want them to be like your girlfriends. A man brings something uniquely male to a woman's life – a complimentary energy but a different one. A secure woman is not looking for an emotional clone, but rather a match for her feminine energy. She knows who she is and does not need a man to see things the same way she does. She enjoys the differences and delights in them.

A wise woman may not need a man, but if she wants one, she will find one.

I Think Celibacy Is The Way To Go.

Deciding you want to be celibate is like taking "there aren't any good men out there" to the next level. You've just upped the ante and erected another wall to feeling connected. Unless you are a sex addict and need the discipline, why would you close yourself off from the possibility of meeting a man, liking him, having sex, and feeling good?

Celibacy only works, in a limited way, when it is true renunciation and not denial. It is so easy to be deceived. You tell yourself sex is overrated, distracting, and that there are other things more important. But if you are honest with yourself, you will admit that all this sex and intimacy stuff is confusing and that you don't do it very well. But "doing it well" takes practice and the only way you will ever get better is to stay in the game.

Remember – feeling something is always better than feeling nothing.

Exercise 5:

Spend The Weekend Alone.
Do Not Make Any Plans.

The key is not only being alone, but also not planning your weekend even if you are.

Begin to get a sense of yourself, again, or perhaps for the first time. Splitting up takes its toll and there is no way not to get weary after a while. Unless you can begin to remember what you like to do, what makes you feel good... you can never even move on to something good and healthy.

Stay alone even if it's scary. Out of the scariness you will find out who you are, and that will give you the strength to begin again.

Reward 5:

Have A Party! Celebrate Yourself!

You have just completed a very brave task and you deserve a party. Anyone who remembers her first night spent alone (and you did an entire weekend) will honor you at your party.

Remember, all women, if they are honest, can tell you a story about being alone. There is no short cut to this process – no way to be alone without actually doing it – no way to be brave without first being scared. It is the same for us all and anyone who tells you differently called a friend to lessen the intensity.

It always begins as a sad story, but it inevitably ends up joyful. Most importantly, you will never be the same. Having survived the night, you celebrate the day!

6. The Right Relationship

Things You Know When It's The "Real Deal":

• You just really like the other person. (The longer you know him, the more you like him.)

• You want to stay, even on days when you do not like him.

• You laugh – a lot.

• You say how you feel, even when it's hard.

• You care about feeling right, not being right.

• You play – a lot.

• You feel he "gets you."

• You feel blessed and honored to be in this relationship.

• You love making him feel good.

• You enjoy being loved.

No Excuses

Exercise 6:

Have A ball!

Reward 6:

A LIFE!

7. Quick 'n Dirty

How To Stop Believing Your Own Excuses And Have A Real Relationship

• Feel – only by feeling can you recognize a match. Thinking will always cut you short.

• Say what makes you feel good, what doesn't. Unless you speak up, no one has the chance to give you what you need.

• Admit when things are messed up. Don't try to cover up garbage by pretending it doesn't exist; everything ends up smelling.

• Pay for professional help if you are stuck, and quit telling your tale of woe to anyone who will listen.

• Stop complaining – it's unattractive and whiny.

• Surround yourself with people who speak the truth and not what you want to hear. Gathering consensus for your point of view only further cements the incongruity between what you are thinking and what you are feeling. You end up being more confused, rather than less.

• Try a new way – maybe you'll get a new result.

• Be a stand-up gal and take responsibility for all of it. If you don't like what you've got, do something to change it. Do not expect it all to "make sense." If it happened to you, it belongs to you.

- Apologize – it saves a lot of time and besides, if your intent was not to hurt, what difference does it make?

- Be brave – forging in a new direction always takes courage.

- Don't make a decision until everything in you says "go." Don't force one because the unknown is scary. This way you will not have to backtrack.

- Recognize recurring patterns even though the package may look different each time.

- Stop believing anger is a bona fide emotion – it is not. Anger is sadness flipped upside down. When we can't feel, we get angry.

- Stop using the past and future as reasons to not stay in the present. Either the present is good enough or it's not.

- Speak up even if you don't have the answer. You don't need to have a solution in order to have a feeling.

- Listen to what you are saying as though you are listening to a friend. If you hear, "Yes...but," tell yourself to stop.

"Yes…but" is always the beginning of a rationalization and never in your best interest.

• Do not act when you hear yourself say, "I really should do this (whatever)." "Should" is always about all those other voices in your head other than your own. It is what you think you should do, and is in direct conflict with how you feel.

• Be vulnerable, even though you are scared. Let someone "see" who you are. Your willingness to be open allows someone else to be. When you wait for the other person to do it first, it never happens.

• Understand that being constantly busy is not the same as having a healthy relationship and a good life.

• Sit quietly every day. A quiet mind is the bedrock of a life without excuses.

About Chandra Alexander, MSW

After graduating from the University of Florida with an undergraduate degree in English and Education, Chandra received her MSW in Social Work from Barry University, with intensive training and experience in traditional psychotherapy and counseling.

Along the way, she developed top-notch business experience, spending years in upper management with an HMO, consulting for General Motor's healthcare division, and developing two start-up companies.

Called "Tampa Bay's own Dr. Phil," Tampa Life Coach Chandra Alexander has a private practice in Tampa, Florida, coaching clients from all over the world (in person, on the phone, and on Skype) in the areas of business, relationships, and consciousness. She has been doing this work for the last 30 years. She has traveled the world, spending ten years in India, studying and meditating with a great spiritual master.

From April 2002 through November 2006, Ms. Alexander had a regular TV series on WFLA/NBC's DAYTIME called "Reality Check." In September 2005, she was selected by *Oprah Magazine* as the Life Coach to deliver 12 coaching sessions to the first-prize winner of their Toyota Moving Forward essay contest. She spent one year on Good Day Tampa Bay/FOX 13 TV with Russell Rhodes and another year on WFLA Channel 8's Midday News with Gayle Guyardo.

Her self-help books and CDs are always about bravery and authenticity. Her first book, *Reality Works, Let It Happen*, is for those who want their spirituality straight-up – bite-sized chapters on what it takes to make the journey authentic.

Her new book, *Relationship Therapy On Demand* is like having a therapist on call. Women will buy this book for one another and men will secretly buy it for themselves. And her book, *EPIPHANY, Power Statements That Change Your Life*, is an opportunity to integrate your insights and transform your consciousness.

Chandra Alexander's CDs correct the focus, and point you inward. *A Working Relationship with the Mind* CD gives you